From Russian P.O.W.

to

Thamesford Ontario

Stanley Omielan

(A Remarkable True Story)

by

Frank Dyer

Published by:
Frank Dyer

Printed in Canada:
JC Graphics, Thamesford
Thumbs Up Publications

ISBN 978-0-9936318-6-3

Published December 2021

The Saga of Stanley O. (A True Story)

Preface

I met Stan Omielan about 1960. He had a small mechanic's garage between Thamesford and Ingersoll, Ontario. He became my mechanic and although I was at least ten years his junior, as the years passed we became very good friends. When he found out that I was teaching physics at a nearby high school, he had all kinds of questions for me. Of course he spoke and read Polish very well, but when he tried to read English language mechanic's journals he became confused. He often wanted me to explain English technical terms, and to help him fill out various government forms. He very quickly caught on to mechanical terms and I considered him very bright, possibly brilliant. When he first started telling me about his early life in Poland and Russia, I was absolutely fascinated. This is a true story as he told it. I have included conversations and some descriptions as I imagined them. Here is the fascinating and almost unbelievable life story of Stanley Omielan.

Frank Dyer

Chapter # 1

German Prisoner-of-War Train

"Stop talking!" the burly German soldier holding a murderous looking sub-machine gun bellowed, in his guttural accent, as my friend, Jon, had hissed trying to get my attention. There were about ten of us, some seated, some standing in this small, old wooden railway car compartment built to hold about six people. We were a rough looking bunch, dirty, unshaven, unwashed, all angry and depressed, all Polish Army prisoners being transported back to Germany after a quick, one sided battle with the mighty German War Machine in September, 1939. We all were aware of the power behind that gun-totting guard.

After a few minutes my friend carefully whispered again, indicating that I should try to distract the guard while he tried to pry open a window. It worked, and after I had been escorted back to my spot from the trip to the "potty", I saw that the window was free and could be opened if an opportunity presented itself. I pretended to sleep as the train rumbled on. I thought of my childhood in the small Polish village of Costto, in central Poland near Warsaw. We were a poor but reasonably happy family. My father, the village blacksmith, was very serious about teaching his two sons everything about blacksmithing as well as the repair and improvement of all types of farmer's machinery that was brought in. As soon as we had finished grade eight, we both helped our father in the shop, but in the last two years my brother and I had established a good little business building bicycles. We bought the wheels and chain from a supplier, and built the rest of the bike from iron pipe, cutting and welding the pipe in father's shop. The bikes were crude and heavy but rugged and cheap.

It irritated us that the only supplier of wheels was a German firm. It seemed that the arrogant Germans completely dominated all the industry in Europe.

My friend coughed again, alerting me that we were slowing down, possibly because of a small hill. A couple of other prisoners had noticed our intentions and had nodded to us indicating that one of them was ready to help when needed. We waited, sweat pouring down our backs, then the moment arrived. Our unknown prisoner friend yelled and fell over on the floor pretending heart attack or something. In the confusion that immediately followed, first my friend and then I, jumped through the open window landing on the ground beside the railway. I landed hard on my shoulder but still managed to roll, then get up and run. And run I did, as fast as I could, straight away from the train across some farmer's fields. I heard the train stop, then loud voices. I saw the bright beams from the guard's big flashlights getting closer, then some shots. Completely out of breath, I dived into a small depression behind some small bushes and tried to be quiet as I watched the guards approaching, then, run on past me.

As I lay there listening to the commotion, I thought back again to my life only a few weeks before. For a couple of years we had heard frightening stories coming out of Germany. Some of our neighbours had left, saying that Poland would soon be overrun. Others said that that would not happen as Poland had made a treaty with Great Britain and was assured of protection. It seemed impossible that it was only two weeks ago that Poland had been attacked and my brother and I had joined the Polish Army. After only about a week of intense training we were rushed off to the front. Although the Polish Army had over a million men, we had little equipment, and it was old and obsolete. My rifle was of the pre-world-war-one type, and had jammed after firing only two shots. I was only in battle a few minutes when captured by the Germans.

Chapter # 2

Freedom

As I lay there shivering on the hard ground, listening to the sound of the train moving on, I tried to plan my next move. I had absolutely no idea where I was. I thought likely I was still in Poland. I had no watch but I estimated that I had been on the train for about ten hours. For some of that time we had been stopped. If we had moved at about twenty kilometers per hour and had been moving for five hours that would mean that I was possibly one hundred kilometers west of the front, certainly several days walk. On the other hand the train possibly was only shunting back and forth and I might still be close to the front. As I carefully got up and looked around in the inky darkness, I managed to locate the North Star, so I turned towards the East and started slowly walking. I was cold and hungry. The German guards had fed us once on the train. We each had been given a couple of slices of heavy black German bread dipped in some kind of stew. We grumbled then about the quality of the food but now almost any kind of food would be welcome. I reasoned that although this was likely German controlled property, any local people would likely be Polish. I realized that I was making a lot of assumptions.

However I was right. As the sky in the east slowly lightened, I saw what appeared to be a small farm house. As I came nearer I could see a tiny light glowing from one window. I decided to sit down and wait. If this was a farmhouse, someone should appear shortly. I was right again. After about a half-hour wait, a man slowly opened the door, let his dog out, stepped out and started walking towards another small building. Suddenly the dog let out a fierce growl, turned, and started running towards me. I immediately stood up, raised my hands, and called out in Polish. "Please help me. I am a Polish soldier, just escaped from a prisoner-of –war train!" The farmer yelled at the dog, who had stopped a few feet in front of me, still growling and snarling. I waited, my heart pounding, to see if the man replied in Polish. He raised his little lantern and called out, thankfully, in Polish.

"Hello there" he said quietly, "Yes I heard the train stop and some shots fired. Are you hurt?" Immensely relived, I replied, "No, I am OK. I am cold and hungry but not hurt." The man raised his hand and motioned for me to follow him to his house. In a few minutes I was seated in his warm little kitchen, bowl of soup in hand telling him my story, then listening as he told me his.

"Well the German army came through here about a week ago. There really was little opposition. I have had a couple of visits, no real threats. I had been supplying the Polish army with hay for their horses. Imagine! The Polish Cavalry, on horseback of course, apparently attacked German tanks! Ridiculous! Now, do you have a plan?" "Well," I answered slowly, "I would like to get back into the Army. But where am I? And how far away is the front?"

The man, who said his name was Joe, laughed. "Actually, I have no idea where the front is. We get very little news. The nearest village is called Jotha. We are about fifty miles from Warsaw. I think Warsaw is still in Polish hands. There has been no action around here for several days. I have a little map here that you can have. However" He stopped for a minute, thinking then continued. "I have an idea. A German sergeant came by yesterday and asked if I could take a load of hay to their base at Gerrno which is about 10 km away. He left me a safe passage note. Apparently they still use horses in the German Army for parades etc. Possibly you could hide under the hay until we get to the Rink River, which is about half way to Gerrno. I think there still is a small Polish Army outpost just down that river. If you are careful, under cover of darkness, I think you could slip, through the bushes alongside the river to the camp." "OK," I replied slowly. "Let's think about that. Firstly, would the Germans not search the hay?" "I have no idea. But I think not likely. They might have dogs, but dogs are useless around hay because the dust and pollen gets up their noses and they start sneezing."

"OK," I replied, then continued, "What about the bridge over the river that you mentioned. Would it not be guarded?" "That is possible but not likely. I was over it yesterday and there was no one around. Of course any movement on your part will be very dangerous, but if you are careful and with a bit of luck I think you might make it. Of course I don't know if there still are any Polish Army men still at that camp. You would have to take that chance."

It happened exactly as he had suggested. I arrived at the Polish camp in the middle of the night, barely managed to convince the guards that I was a genuine Pole, then, joined them in their frantic preparations to withdraw to Warsaw.

We arrived in Warsaw a couple of days later and found that incredibly, Hitler and Stalin had signed a non-aggression agreement and now the Russian army was invading Poland from the East! Since I was now considered an old Army veteran, I was promoted to Sergeant, assigned to a new outfit, and sent east immediately try to stop the Russians.

Chapter # 3

On a Russian Prisoner-of-War Train

"Stop Talking!" This time it was a big 250 lb guard who growled at us as we were herded aboard a large box car. It really seemed like a bad dream. Only a week ago I was a prisoner on a German train headed west, now I was a prisoner on a Russian train headed east! This time rather than being overcrowded in a small rail coach guarded by a German soldier, a large number of us, I don't know how many, were crowded into a large railway car, possibly previously used to carry grain or lumber. When the huge door was slammed shut with a crash, there was no way of escape. A guard was not needed. Almost immediately the train started moving, and as I looked about in the semi-darkness, I recognized some of my fellow soldiers.

I remembered well the previous night. As our loaded Polish troop train carrying a whole company of soldiers had left Warsaw, we were in high spirits. This time we would not be fighting with obsolete old guns and equipment. Our officers had told us that a whole shipment of brand new equipment had arrived from England and was packed in several cars at the end of the train. We cheered as they told us that as soon as we reached the combat area we would be issued this equipment and we would take on the Russians who had invaded our ancestral home from the east. As the train thundered on through the night towards the enemy we were in a great mood. We laughed and sang as we talked about former army experiences.

Then suddenly there was a huge crash as the train brakes came on, and the train slowly ground to a halt. As we peered out into the darkness, to our horror we could see hundreds of armed Russian soldiers lining the ditches. We were ordered out. There was nothing else that we could do. Our new rifles and other arms were securely locked away in the baggage cars at the end of the train. Apparently the front was much closer than expected and we had been ambushed by the Russians. We were quickly lined up and marched several miles to a waiting Russian train.

As this train lurched forward, amid much yelling, grumbling and swearing, we began to examine our new surroundings. They certainly were very depressing. From the little bit of light that came through the holes in the roof we could see that we were quite crowded, some standing and some sitting. On examination I found that there was a large tub at one corner, filled with water, apparently to be used for drinking as there was also a cup hanging by a chain. In the far corner there was another low tub, apparently to be used as a latrine. That was all. Initially there was a great deal of confusion and shouting as it seemed that our officers had all been confined to another car but then a man who claimed to be a captain finally got the men's attention. He stood on some kind of platform and asked for all the non-commissioned officers to gather around him and they would try to make some plans. They first asked for anyone who was ill to come forward, but no one did. We were all young healthy men. The speaker then talked for some time, asking us to try to remain calm, saying that we really had no idea about our destination, likely deep inside Russia, and that hopefully we would stop soon to eat as we had had nothing to eat since the previous night. The train rumbled on.

After what seemed like several hours the train did slow down and stop. We waited rather impatiently for another hour or so then the door locks were released and the large doors opened a few feet to reveal several stubby machine gun- armed guards and a Polish speaking Russian officer just outside. He told us that we were now prisoners in the hands of the Russian Army and we had nothing to fear if we did as instructed. He also pointed out that we were in the middle of a vast level field so there could be no escape. He continued that we should now quietly climb out and begin lining up at the field kitchen for some food. As we jumped down from the train we could see our fellow soldiers exiting from the other cars, also a great circle of armed guards around the whole train. There would be little chance of escape here! Then as we started for the food area we realized that there were several hundred Polish prisoners and only one food kitchen. Some of us would be in line for several hours! However although certainly very apprehensive about our future, it felt good just to stretch and line up for the possibility of food. The Russians appeared to be well organized. They had stopped the train near a small growth of old trees, so there was ample dry wood for cooking. A hot fire was burning under three huge kettles, each probably holding a hundred gallons of thick, stew like soup. Fortunately I was close to the front of the line and was told to hurry up, then was handed a spoon, a deep metal dish, and a large thick slice of black bread. A cook's helper filled my dish and yelled "pusheet" (hurry up). Certainly it was primitive, but the soup also was hot and thick, probably containing horse meat, and it was fast. After eating, we washed the spoon and bowl in another large tub and laid them on a large sheet to dry. I suppose we were stopped for only a couple of hours. Then ordered back into the train and we continued on.

This became the pattern. We stopped every six or seven hours for a remarkably similar food break, sometimes the soup would be augmented with milk or fruit from nearby farms, then back into the train. We had no idea where we were or where we were going. After a couple of days we noticed the weather tuning colder so we assumed that we were heading north, probably to Siberia. By now it was early October and although some of us had our heavy army jackets, feeling the cold was another of our discomforts. Escape appeared impossible. Early in the trip a couple of prisoners tried to make a run for it but were immediately shot and left to rot as the rest of us were herded back into the train. The guards were grim and surly but as long as we did as we were told, did not purposely harm anyone.

Finally after, what we estimated was ten days on the train, we stopped and once again waited for several hours before being allowed out. We stepped out into a large stump filled clearing that seemed to be in a thick woods. In the distance was some kind of large building. Of course we immediately noted the ring of grim looking armed guards surrounding us. After much shouting and yelling we moved to an area near a platform on which stood several Russian officers. A Polish speaking officer finally got our attention and began an hour long speech.

He told us that we were in Russian Siberia, and that we would be employed in a logging camp. We were deep in the woods with winter coming on so that there was absolutely no possibility of escape. He continued that what we had considered Poland was really part of Mother Russia, and had only been separated as a state, by the Central Powers after the first World War. We would be well treated if we worked hard and did as instructed. He finished on a sombre note. They had no medical facilities and the sick would simply be shot and buried. By this time it was dark so we were then moved over to the familiar field kitchen for a meal, and then into the very large log building. This building held about one hundred prisoners, had a huge fire going in the centre, with some smoke going out a large hole in the roof, and simply a foot or so of straw on the ground for us to sleep on. It was indeed a very dismal prospect.

Chapter # 4

The Logging Camp

The next month was probably the worst time in my life. It immediately became apparent to me that very few of us would survive in these conditions. The Russians worked us very hard for all the daylight hours, that is from about nine in the morning till three in the afternoon. We spent the rest of the time trying to keep warm in the large log building. So in the daytime we were exhausted and at night freezing cold. However by far the most disturbing problem was inadequate food. We were fed twice a day but the slice of bread and bowl of soup was simply not enough and we all soon began showing signs of starvation. I told myself again and again that I would have to do something to change the situation or I would simply die in this utterly terrible camp. What could I do? Complaining to the guards was less than useful, it simply resulted in a beating or other punishment. Escape appeared impossible. Already several prisoners had been shot for disobeying orders. Many were ill and most were becoming desperate. What could I do?

My opportunity came one cold morning as I was working with group of prisoners who had been issued with axes and large hand saws for cutting down the trees and cutting them into logs. Another man then fastened a chain to the log and a team of horses pulled it to a log pile near the railroad tracks. Later it would be loaded on a car for delivery to a sawmill some distance away. On this morning a minor accident had occurred. As the horses were pulling a large log it caught on a stump and the chain broke. After much yelling and shouting the guard had called an officer, apparently to discipline the driver of the horses. I recognized the officer as the Polish speaking one that had spoken to us before. I hurried over and very politely told the officer that I was a blacksmith and, given the tools could fix the chain. He looked at me silently for a minute or so then and said, "OK, we had better have a talk." That saved my life. As far as I know I would become the only survivor from that first whole train load of prisoners.

The officer and I sat down on a log and talked for some time. The officer said that they had had several chains broken as well as several broken saws and axes. He knew that they could be repaired. He wanted to know what I would need to set up a shop and start working. Initially he got me some coal from the railroad, a couple of big hammers, some iron rod, and told me I had a half day to fix the chain. He assigned me a helper and we went to work. A half day later the chain was fixed and the officer was very pleased.

That was the beginning of a huge change in my situation. Now I was considered a skilled trades-man with many privileges, most important of which was a double ration of food. I was given several helpers and we began immediately to fabricate our blacksmith tools. A veritable mountain of broken tools started to come in from the various camps. As I tried to repair some of the essential broken items with our primitive tools, the others began building a large foot-driven bellows and a large forge. We were very pleased at the prospect of steady work in a very much better atmosphere. Initially we worked in a simple lean-to that protected us from the wind and snow then as the work continued to come in we started construction of a larger building with sleeping room for all of us and a large room for the blacksmith operation. In a short time I was fixing all manner of things from broken chains to broken or bent soup ladles from the kitchen. One very welcome result was that whenever a broken tool was brought from the kitchen for repair, usually a bit of food was included. On one occasion they brought me a broken part of locomotive. I worked on that for several days before returning it apparently fixed to their satisfaction. Of course another benefit was that we were able to sleep in a warm private building. I immediately began teaching my helpers the blacksmith trade. The

Russians were pleased with our work and gradually we were given a good deal of independence and relative freedom.

After the first rush of broken tools, another source of work appeared. There were several hundred workers cutting logs with axes and saws. As well as these tools being broken on occasion, each one needed to be sharpened regularly. Soon I had a couple of men simply sharpening saws all day long. Wooden axe handles broke on occasion. Although really not a blacksmith's job, soon we had a couple of men making new axe handles. The rest of that year was much better than the first half.

Chapter # 5

Historical Note: On August 14, 1941 a Polish-Russian agreement was signed granting amnesty to Poles in Russia and also allowing the formation of a Polish Army on Russian soil. Initially this Army was to fight alongside the Russian Army, however in September 1942, because of lack of support from Russia, the Polish Army known as Anders Army after its commander, General Anders, was transferred to the British Army. Stanley was a Lance-Corporal in Anders Army.

Escape from Slavery

In camp we had no authentic source of information. Of course rumours swirled around camp continually about the German conquest of Europe and even the conquest of England, but we all knew that this information was very suspect. About every six weeks or so the Communist Political Commissioner would give a lecture on the benefits of communism and its eventual supremacy in the world, but little actual news. On occasion a trainload of prisoners would stop at our camp for food, and we would get a little information from the outside world. Then in summer of 1941 this changed.

Roll call each morning had become a standard routine. We would all stand at attention while being counted and reports of sick or deceased prisoners were submitted. Generally it had become an irritating but a well organized operation. However on this morning it was very different. As we slowly lined up we noticed that initially there were no guards yelling and shouting at us. When they did appear they were obviously very excited, almost ignoring us, yelling and shouting to each other. Finally an officer appeared and mounting a platform, asked for our attention.

"Men of camp number seventeen," he shouted. "Can I have your attention?" We were all quite surprised as we had never been addressed as 'men' before, always as 'prisoners'.

The officer continued, "This morning we have just received the news that The German Army has invaded the Soviet Union! This is a complete surprise to us. The report states that the Germans are attacking on a very wide front. Of course the men of our great Russian Army are fighting heroically but are vastly outnumbered. We estimate that there were at least a hundred thousand men captured from the Polish Army. In view of this military development the authorities have decided to grant amnesty to all Polish personal and to allow the formation of a Polish Army. This Army will fight alongside the great Russian Army. I will call another meeting tomorrow to answer any questions."

Of course when we returned to our bunk houses there was a great deal of very hot discussions. Some said that they would die before they would join the Russian Army. Some pointed out that there were very few able-bodied men in camp. Most were in very poor shape due to malnutrition. For myself I already had a double food ration because of my blacksmith skill. However in the end it made no difference. In the morning we were all lined up, loaded into a train and on our way to a large camp near Moscow. Here we were separated into able-bodied and non-able bodied. The non able-bodied were sent to a rehabilitation camp and the rest of us were organized under Polish officers and our new training began.

However once again I was enormously fortunate. Most of the men from the able-bodied camp were sent for a short course in the use of guns, or basic army tactics, etc, then off to the front. Because of my work as a blacksmith I was considered skilled and was sent to a huge army training and repair shop just east of Moscow. Here Russian army trucks and tanks that had been damaged at the front were repaired and rebuilt. We were worked extremely hard, often fifteen or more hours per day. However we had adequate food, a warm bunk at night and for me the work was quite interesting. I had an excellent instructor and we got along well. I remember one incident. Apparently Russian officials had conferred with American officials and had agreed on a massive Lend-lease arrangement whereby the Americans would supply some equipment to the Russian Army. There was great excitement one day at the repair shop as an American truck had been brought in for repair. This was the very first American equipment that we had seen. Here was a huge six-wheel drive Studebaker truck, much larger than any of ours and even larger than some German trucks that we had worked on. It had a massive six cylinder engine, with a large roomy cab and even to our astonishment a large cab heater! Initially we could not understand the use for a removable, little electric heater in the cab. Finally someone suggested that it was a cigarette lighter!

I worked for over a year in that shop and learned a great deal. However once again fate took a hand and my life changed enormously.

Chapter # 6

A Change for the Better.

"Hey Stan, have you heard the news?" A fellow Polish mechanic shouted as I, with a half dozen or so of my group, struggled to replace a heavy section of track on a big Russian tank.

"What is the gossip now?" I replied. There was a constant flow of rumours, some quite ridiculous, that went around camp. Since I had now been in Russia for more than two years, I could understand to some extent the Russian language and could often overhear the officers talking, so I knew a little bit about what was going on outside our camp.

"No gossip this time Stan. The news is that we are going to join the British Army!"

Indeed, although this seemed utterly unlikely, it turned out to be true. From time to time our Russian overseer had given a news conference. This generally was about the activities of the Great Russian Army but also some world news. We knew that the war was going very badly for the allies. The Germans were regularly sinking huge convoys of American men and materials in the North Atlantic. Even in North Africa, the German General Rommel was pushing the British Army back, and also that despite Russia committing enormous amounts of men and material, and suffering great losses, the German Army was still relentlessly advancing towards Moscow. Apparently Stalin was putting pressure on the Allies to increase their fight against the Germans so as to take some pressure off Russia. One result was that in September 1942 the Russian leaders had agreed to release the Polish Army to the British Army if they would be then fighting the Germans.

This of course was great news for us. We had no idea as to how we would get from Moscow to England, as that is where we thought we would be going. However, England was not our destination. Instead, in an amazingly short time, only a few days, I was on board a slowly moving Russian train heading for the Middle East, to Iran. Apparently the British were keeping a strong force in the area to deny it to the Germans. A couple of days later we all slowly emerged from the train on a hot day to face a big burly British Staff Sergeant shouting orders in English. Darn, I thought, first, a long time ago, I learned to understand Polish army orders, then later Russian speech, now I had to learn English! However in a short time we were all lined up and an interpreter was describing our new life and apparently new training schedule.

It turned out that this life was a great deal different from life in Russia. In the next couple of weeks train after train arrived bringing Polish army personnel. At first we were called simply Anders Army, named for our Polish Army commander, then later five complete Infantry divisions were formed, complete with Polish officers. Of course the soldier's pay and cost of equipment all came from the British Treasury. To us this was a wonderful change. Not only was the food and lodgings much better, but we were all treated as honest men if not actual heroes of the great Polish Army. We spent a good deal of time in the Middle East, training and organizing before we were sent West to join the British 8th Army, that was suffering huge losses as they tried to push the Germans out of Italy. We were very proud to be part of this great endeavour. Interestingly, I now had become part of the Polish Infantry, attached to the British Army, driving American built trucks!

Trying to fight in the rain and mud of northern Italy that winter was difficult beyond description. In January 1944 the Polish Division was ordered to attack the great German stronghold of Monte Cassino. Several other British Units had attempted and failed. However despite terrible losses The 1st Polish Division received international acclaim as we were finally able to drive the Germans out. We continued to fight with the British 8th Army, capturing Rome in June '44, then continuing through northern Italy. I was part of the Polish 5th Infantry Division with the British 8th Army til the end of the war in April 1945. The Corps was part of the occupation in Italy until 1946. I was demobilized in September 1946.

As the war drew to a close, there was a great deal of discussion in all levels of the Polish Army as to what would happen to us after the war. Would we simply be released to return to war devastated Poland, or could we immigrate to some other country? Then, in mid 1946 Britain issued a remarkable offer. Anyone who had served with the British Army could move to any part of the British Empire and receive full citizenship. I chose Canada!

Chapter # 7

Life in Canada

"Hey, it is time to get up you lazy bum! You can't sleep in on a farm like you did in the army!", shouted my Canadian farmer boss every morning about 5:00 am.

After arriving in Canada, in late fall of 1946, I had found out that the Canadian Authorities had placed conditions on British ex-army personal who wished to become Canadian citizens. One condition was that one must work for a farmer for the first two years. I was sent to a farm just north of London, Ontario. Here the conditions were very poor. By this time I could understand English reasonably well, but still had trouble speaking it. My farmer-boss worked me very hard generally from 5:00 a.m. til 9:00 p.m. with only a few breaks. He was constantly yelling obscenities at me, which I could understand, and telling me to work harder and faster.

However the worst part was the food and accommodations. I was not allowed to eat with the family. Henry, my boss, would bring me my meals on a plate so I could eat in the yard, or in the garage if the weather was bad. The food was quite insufficient, so I quickly became very hungry. I found out that my pay was $2 per day and I could have Saturday afternoon off. Consequently I would walk into town on Saturday, buy a couple of loaves of bread and a large package of wieners to take back to eat during the week. My sleeping arrangement was also very poor. I was given a small room above the garage, with one little window and almost no heating. I had arrived in mid October so initially

I was warm enough at night. However this changed as the Canadian winter approached.

Very fortunately I had, quite by chance made a friend. One Saturday, while in town, I was approached by a Catholic priest who spoke to me in Polish! Although I was not religious, he became my salvation! We became good friends and this friendship continued the rest of my life. His church had a community help program, and soon clothing, blankets and even food became available to me. I was very thankful. On one occasion my friend drove out to the farm to see me. Henry, my boss, met him in the yard and ordered him off the property. He told me that if he ever saw him again at the farm he would call the police and report me to some authority.

"Stanley", he called one morning, I think possibly in March or April. "We have to have a little talk!" I was very surprised at this because so far it had been all yelling and no talking.

"I have just got a notice that an inspector of some kind is coming tomorrow. Now be careful about what you say to him. Remember if there is a difference between what I say and what you say, of course he will believe me. So be careful!"

I need not have worried. The inspector apparently from the Govt Immigration Dept said very little to me. As I had been instructed, I sat in an adjoining room, in my best clothes, waiting. Presently I could overhear the conversation. Henry and the inspector became increasingly loud as they laughed and talked about the problems these DPs (Displaced Persons) that were coming over from Europe, were causing. His questions to the farmer were mostly about whether I was working hard enough. However as he was leaving he said something very important to me.

"You know that you are obligated to work for this good farmer for only a year. Next year you can choose another one if you wish." Wow! I sure would try!

When I told my friend the priest, he immediately said that he could find me a much better place to work. So one Saturday in the summer he drove me to a farm near St. Thomas and introduced me to my next boss. I was very impressed and excited. He seem to be a very friendly, sensible man. He introduced me to his wife and two young boys. I looked forward to the change.

On the first of September my friend drove me to my new place of employment. Wow! what a difference it turned out to be. I was given a beautiful little room with a chest of drawers and a bed with a real mattress! I ate with the friendly family and the food was simply great. I still worked hard, getting up at 5:00 a.m., to milk cows but I didn't mind that. We generally finished work about 6:00 p.m. Really what I liked best was that they wanted me to be part of the family. I spent many long evenings discussing Canadian customs and society. We all laughed when I made mistakes as I tried to learn the English language. Canada was much different from my native Poland.

As the year went on, my boss Dave, wanted to know what I wanted to do next year. When I told him that I thought I would like to be an auto mechanic, he generously offered to get the necessary information and papers. I found that I had to work for a licensed mechanic for five years and write several examinations. I knew I would have trouble with the exams, in English, but first I had to find a mechanic that would hire me and help me learn the trade.

So I began my search for a new place of employment. Dave suggested that first I should get my Canadian drivers permit. Driving was not a problem as I had been driving tanks, trucks and army vehicles for years. Learning the meaning of the English road signs, and highway driving rules was another matter. However my farm boss Dave, was a good teacher and I successfully tried and passed the driving exam. I was very pleased and proud!

Chapter # 8

Life at Thamesford, Ontario.

My very first real job in Canada came about largely by good fortune. My friend the good Canadian farmer, very generously had driven me around the area looking for a garage that would hire me. We found that few were interested in hiring an inexperienced man, who really could not speak English. One day we stopped at a little garage about five miles east of London and began talking to the owner. While there we noticed another mechanic who was working unsuccessfully on an old farm tractor trying to get it started. By the rarest of chances, I had worked on a very similar tractor in Russia, a one cylinder, English made tractor. I offered to start the tractor. The mechanic laughed and said, "Sure go ahead!" In a couple of minutes the tractor was running! The owner of the shop immediately offered me a job. This was the start of several very good years working at Pelton's Garage. Mr. Grant Pelton the owner operator, was sensible and fair. We got along well, we even exchanged presents at Christmas time. I remember one Christmas the evident glee of their eight-year old son when he opened his present from me, a cowboy shirt. However when a new General Motors dealership opened in Thamesford, and advertised for mechanics, I applied and started work there.

This new move proved to be a big mistake. Although the owner, Mr John Wright, was an excellent boss, and we got along very well, I could not get along with one of the men working there. We constantly disagreed, sometimes quite seriously. The result was that when a small garage a few miles east of Thames-ford, at a little place called Dickson's Corners, came up for sale, Mr. Wright helped me make arrangements to buy it. It was an excellent choice, although there was little equipment in the garage, it included a large lot and two storey house. Customers started coming immediately. I was very pleased with my new enterprise.

Ever since the end of the war, I had been trying to contact my Polish family. There were several organizations based in Europe that worked to try to reunite people displaced by the war. These organizations periodically published long lists of the names of people trying to contact someone else. I did not know if any of my family had even survived. Then in the early fifties I got a letter from my brother! It was great to hear from him, however I learned that unfortunately, apparently he was the only survivor. We immediately exchanged many letters telling each other about what had happened since we last saw each other. I tried very hard to persuade him to attempt to emmigrate to Canada. He absolutely refused to leave Poland, and although very happy to learn of my good life in Canada, was concerned that I did not have a wife! We exchanged many letters, then he wrote that he had found the perfect woman for me. He wanted me to come immediately to Poland to meet and marry her.

That is exactly what I did. I made arrangements to take a two week holiday. I flew to Poland, and met my brother. He and I mounted bicycles and rode to a nearby village where I was introduced to my brother's choice for me. Near the end of the second week we had a small wedding, and then my new wife and I flew home.

Shortly after we got back to Thamesford, much to the surprise of both my new wife and I, my former employer, Mr Grant Pelton and family, organized a wonderful party for us at their home. Besides the Pelton family, many of my new Canadian acquaintances, including my priest friend, attended the party. We were very pleased and thankful.

For the next several years my auto-repair business prospered, so when the opportunity came, I purchased a large lot across the road and proceeded to build a new house. This was quite a new endeavour for me, as I had never worked in the construction industry. However I had good advice and help from several of my Canadian friends, so that both my wife and family, I now had three sons, were very pleased with the result. My next project was to build a new shop. I built it so that it was both a repair shop and a machine shop with a large industrial lathe and vertical mill. While in the Russian Army, working in their huge vehicle repair shop I had developed a good deal of machine-shop skill. I liked this kind of work and found that there was a good deal of demand for machine work in this farming community.

When my youngest son Walter, was about ten years old, he and I went back to Poland for a wonderful two week visit.

My boys have done well in school, all three now have advanced university degrees and good jobs. I am happy here in this community with my shop work.

The End

Note: Stanley developed cancer and passed away in 1990.

BALTIC
SEA

Łeba · Władysławowo · Kaliningrad
Ustka · Gdynia RUSSIA LITHUANIA
Słupsk · Sopot · Gdańsk
Kołobrzeg · Koszalin Elbląg · Bartoszyce Suwałki
54° Bytów · Kościerzyna WARMIŃSKO-MAZURSKIE Olecko
Świnoujście · Tczew Malbork Mrągowo · Augustów Hrodna
ZACHODNIO- · Świdwin · Czersk POMORSKIE Olsztyn · Pisz
POMORSKIE Szczecinek · Iława Sokółka
Szczecin · Złocieniec Tuchola Lubawa Nidzica Kolno PODLASKIE
Stargard KUJAWSKO- Grudziądz Łomża
Pyrzyce · Szczeciński Piła Bydgoszcz · POMORSKIE Mława · Ostrołęka Białystok
Gorzów · Toruń Ciechanów Zambrów
Wielkopolski Inowrocław · Hajnówka
Gniezno Włocławek Pułtusk
GERMANY Kostrzyn · Mogilno Płock Siemiatycze
LUBUSKIE Poznań POLAND · Gostynin Warsaw BELARUS
Świebodzin Konin · Łęczyca · Siedlce · Brest
52° WIELKOPOLSKIE Turek MAZOWIECKIE Biała
Zielona Góra · Leszno Kalisz Łódź Skierniewice Garwolin Podlaska
Cottbus Nowa Sól Pabianice · Tomaszów Parczew
Głogów Ostrów Sieradz ŁÓDZKIE Mazowiecki Puławy
Wielkopolski Piotrków Radom Chełm
Bolesławiec Legnica Oleśnica Bełchatów · Trybunalski Lublin LUBELSKIE
DOLNOŚLĄSKIE Wrocław Skarżysko-Kamienna Starachowice
Jelenia Świdnica Częstochowa Ostrowiec
Góra Wałbrzych OPOLSKIE Kielce Świętokrzyski Zamość
Kłodzko Opole ŚWIĘTOKRZYSKIE
50° Prague Zabrze Bytom Pińczów Tarnobrzeg Biłgoraj
Gliwice · Dąbrowa Górnicza PODKARPACKIE Lubaczów
Katowice · Sosnowiec Rzeszów
Rybnik Tychy Kraków Tarnów Przemyśl Lviv
Wodzisław Śląski
Ostrava Bielsko-Biała MAŁO- Krosno UKRAINE
CZECH Żywiec POLSKIE Nowy
REPUBLIC Sącz
Zakopane
SLOVAKIA
© 2008 Encyclopædia Britannica, Inc.

Time Line

1939, Aug 23:   Germany (Hitler) and Russia (Stalin) signed an agreement concerning the conquest of Poland. They agreed on the final dividing line between the two forces.

1939, Sept 01:   Germany invaded Poland from the west.

1939, Sept 17:   Russia invaded Poland from the east.

1941, June 22:   Germany invaded Russia.

1941, August 14:   Russia granted amnesty to all poles, prisoners and civilians, and allowed the formation of a Polish Army on Soviet soil. General Anders was appointed commander.

1942, Sept: Polish Army transferred to the command of British Army in the Middle East.

1944, Feb: Polish army transferred to Italy as part of British 8th Army.

1944, May: Polish army captured Monte Casino. (Stanley awarded the
M.C. Medal)

1944, Sept: Polish army fought at Ancona, Italy.

1946, Sept: Stanley demobilised.

OMIELAN, Czeslawa
Apr. 30, 1932 - Sep. 2, 2019

Omielan, Czeslawa passed away unexpectedly on Sep., 2, 2019 in Peace Arch Hospital, White Rock, BC, at the age of 87. She is survived by her sons Joe, John and Walt. She worked hard to raise and support her children as she thought was best. Mass was held in Vancouver, with a graveside service at 10 a.m., Sep. 23 at St. Mary's Roman Catholic Cemetery, 584872 Beachville Rd., Woodstock, ON. Condolences for the family may be left at http://www.kearneyfs.com.

Original location as seen in 2020

House & shop that Stanley built across the road as seen in 2020

www.ingramcontent.com/pod-product-compliance
Lightning Source LLC
Chambersburg PA
CBHW060101050426
42448CB00011B/2574